CW00738927

PHILIP NERI

THE LIGHT OF HOLY JOY

by
Fr Jerome Bertram

*All booklets are published thanks to the
generous support of the members of the
Catholic Truth Society*

CATHOLIC TRUTH SOCIETY
PUBLISHERS TO THE HOLY SEE

CONTENTS

SAINT PHILIP NERI

Saint Philip Neri, one of the best-loved saints of Europe, has inspired the devotion of Catholics and unbelievers, saints and sinners alike; characters as diverse as Pius XII and Paul VI, Goethe and Robespierre, Saint Francis de Sales and Saint Luigi Scrosoppi, Cardinal Newman and John Evelyn have fallen under his spell, even if some did succeed in shrugging off his influence and declining his invitation to holiness. What is it about this man, who lived such a simple life, never stirring far from his 'one bare cell', that evokes such widespread admiration - and so few imitators? And who are these strange imitators, the Fathers and Brothers of the Oratory? It was our own John Henry Newman who described St Philip in a series of evocative phrases, which we may use as our guide in the search for an understanding of the Saint, and, through him, of his sometimes extraordinary followers.

The Litany of St Philip

Lord, have mercy	*Lord, have mercy.*
Christ, have mercy	*Christ, have mercy.*
Lord, have mercy	*Lord, have mercy.*
Christ, hear us	*Christ, graciously hear us.*
God the Father of heaven	*Have mercy on us.*
God the Son, Redeemer of the World,	*Have mercy on us.*
God the Holy Ghost,	*Have mercy on us.*
Holy Trinity, One God,	*Have mercy on us.*
Holy Mary,	*Pray for us.*
Holy Mother of God,	*Pray for us.*
Holy Virgin of Virgins,	*Pray for us.*
St Philip,	*Pray for us.*
Vessel of the Holy Ghost,	*Pray for us.*
Child of Mary,	*Pray for us.*
Apostle of Rome,	*Pray for us.*
Counsellor of Popes,	*Pray for us.*
Voice of prophecy,	*Pray for us.*
Man of primitive times,	*Pray for us.*
Winning saint,	*Pray for us.*
Hidden hero,	*Pray for us.*
Sweetest of Fathers,	*Pray for us.*
Flower of purity,	*Pray for us.*
Martyr of charity,	*Pray for us.*
Heart of fire,	*Pray for us.*
Discerner of spirits,	*Pray for us.*

Choicest of priests,	*Pray for us.*
Mirror of the divine life,	*Pray for us.*
Pattern of humility,	*Pray for us.*
Example of simplicity,	*Pray for us.*
Light of holy joy,	*Pray for us.*
Image of childhood,	*Pray for us.*
Picture of old age,	*Pray for us.*
Director of souls,	*Pray for us.*
Gentle guide of youth,	*Pray for us.*
Patron of thine own,	*Pray for us.*

Who didst observe chastity in thy youth,
Pray for us.
Who didst seek Rome by divine guidance,
Pray for us.
Who didst hide so long in the Catacombs,
Pray for us.
Who didst receive the Holy Ghost into thy heart,
Pray for us.
Who didst experience such wonderful exstacies,
Pray for us.
Who didst so lovingly serve the little ones,
Pray for us.
Who didst wash the feet of pilgrims,
Pray for us.
Who didst ardently thirst after martyrdom,
Pray for us.

Who didst distribute the daily word of God,
Pray for us.
Who didst turn so many hearts to God,
Pray for us.
Who didst converse so sweetly with Mary,
Pray for us.
Who didst raise the dead,
Pray for us.
Who didst set up thy houses in all lands,
Pray for us.
Lamb of God, who takest away the sins of the world,
Spare us, O Lord.
Lamb of God, who takest away the sins of the world,
Graciously hear us, O Lord.
Lamb of God, who takest away the sins of the world,
Have mercy on us.
Christ, hear us
Christ, graciously hear us.

V Remember thy Congregation,
R *Which thou hast possessed from the beginning.*

Let us pray: O God, who hast exalted blessed Philip, thy Confessor, in the glory of thy saints, grant that, as we rejoice in his commemoration, so we may profit by the example of his virtues, through Christ our Lord.
R *Amen.*

THE CHARACTER OF SAINT PHILIP

Vessel of the Holy Ghost

Newman begins by calling him the **Vessel of the Holy Ghost**. You might think that every Christian has a right to that title, and so indeed we do, but St Philip seems to have been conscious of the action of the Holy Ghost - the Holy Spirit - more than most. It is true that there were times when many Christians have all but ignored the Third Person of the Holy Trinity, mentioned him in making the sign of the Cross, of course, and in the Glory Be, but without thinking very much about what it means to say that the Spirit who dwells in our hearts is true God, equal and consubstantial with the Father and the Son. But from time to time a wave of fervour sweeps over the Church, and people suddenly become aware of the power and activity of the Spirit in their lives. St Philip lived in such a time. It is the Holy Spirit who teaches us to pray, the same Spirit who guides our understanding of what is true and what is right, the same Spirit who enables us to do great things, even extraordinary things. All this we can see in the life of Saint Philip and his followers. He had a great gift of prayer, able to remain motionless for hours, totally absorbed in the love of God. And like all genuine men of prayer, he had the ability to transmit that love to others: Tarugi, one of the many young men who were brought, more or less unwillingly, to consult him about their lives, found himself, to his dismay, invited to pray with St Philip - and to his astonishment found that an hour of contemplation in Philip's company 'seemed but a minute'. Saint Philip also had an instinctive ability to distinguish true and false doctrine, to discern the proper way to behave. Not that we should underestimate his application to study: he did follow lectures in theology and philosophy at the Roman schools in his early twenties, and he did read the standard works of Christian doctrine. But his awareness of the truth was internal rather than external; he was soon able to dispense with his books, passing them on to help needy younger students, and without difficulty was able to pick his way through the tangled religious controversies of his age. Newman writes in depth (e.g. in the *Grammar of Assent*) about this instinctive appreciation of the truth, both about faith and morals, which he attributes to the 'illative sense', or 'conscience' or simply the voice of the Holy Spirit in the silence of our hearts. Saint Philip was also a man of action: the Spirit gave him the energy and the ability to organise great works of charity, not only being helpful himself but also inspiring others to do the same. One of his particular fields of activity was in the squalid hospitals of Rome, where he brought his followers to work, to the extent that one of his young men, Saint Camillus de Lellis, dedicated his life to hospital work and founded a great religious order, under the badge of the red cross, to continue that ministry.

Child of Mary

Philip was also the **Child of Mary**. He lived at a time when many were in doubt about the proper degree of honour to be shown to Our Lady - Philip was in no doubt. He accepted Our Lord's dying gift of his Mother to be the mother of the Beloved Disciple, and called on her, trusting her, confiding in her, as his true 'Mamma'. His earthly mother had died when he was a mere child, and he lived far from his remaining family, but in Our Lady he found all the mothering he could desire. And again, he was eager to spread his love and devotion - 'Little children', he would say, 'be attentive to Mary'; in his old age when dying he called out in longing, 'O my Madonna, my beautiful Madonna!' When he was able to build a new church for his work, he was delighted that it stood on the site and preserved the name of the old church of Santa Maria in Vallicella, a title which Newman translated literally when he first became a Catholic and gathered his followers at a house dedicated to Mary of the Vale. Churches of Philip and Newman's institute world-wide have been dedicated to Our Lady under different titles, the Immaculate Conception in Birmingham, the Holy Name of Mary in London.

Apostle of Rome

More unusually, Saint Philip was also called the **Apostle of Rome**, a title you might think pre-empted by St Peter. But Rome in Saint Philip's time was sorely in need of reconversion. Soon before he arrived there, in 1527, it had been laid waste by Imperial troops, and to begin with the shock seemed to stimulate some reform of life and manners. But such shocks soon wear off, and the people and clergy of the Holy City quickly returned to their life of frivolous selfishness. It was an age of corruption, which took the form (as it always does) of allowing the world to set the standard for the Church. Popes and cardinals lived exactly like rich laymen of their class, and rich laymen perpetuated the abuse by arrogating the right to appoint cardinals and Popes. The powerful families of Italy took it in turns to seat one of their members on the throne of Peter, expecting him to reward them by granting ecclesiastical posts (and the salaries attached) to whomever they pleased. The resulting monsignors, bishops, archbishops and cardinals were pleasure-loving youths, who made no attempt whatever to carry out the pastoral and spiritual duties attached to their titles, nor even to reside in the cities or parishes from which they absorbed their funds. That all this changed during the sixteenth century was to a surprising extent the work of Philip. Not that he set out to be a reformer - there were plenty of others doing that, with little success. He did not run about the streets shouting, 'to hell with the adulterers', like the Theatines, but by his quiet example, prayer and spiritual direction, he successfully changed the hearts of the young men who flocked to him until they actually wanted to be good. When they grew up and took their place in Roman society they preserved their attachment to Philip and his teaching, and gradually infiltrated the establishment until Christian morals and charity became as widespread as they had formerly been rare, even in the Curia, the Papal court. The great Council of Trent, which was in session during Philip's first decades in Rome, issued decrees demanding a return to Gospel standards, particularly for the clergy, proclaiming the freedom for the Church to appoint her own bishops, and the duty of those bishops to reside in their sees and use their revenue for the good of their people. But there was great resistance, both on the part of the secular powers and on the part of the bishops themselves. It took the often heroic actions of a small group of dedicated reformers to put the decrees of Trent into effect. The greatest of them was undoubtedly St Charles Borromeo - ironically given his bishopric for the scandalous reason that he was a favourite nephew of the duke - and St Charles was one of St Philip's greatest admirers. Admittedly Charles and Philip quarrelled sharply over whether St Philip should send some of his followers to Milan, but their affection for each other, and their admiration of each other, survived the quarrel. Charles was a man of decisive action; Philip a gentle preacher, but one inspired the other, and St Charles' reforms in Milan became the standard for the world. There was still opposition, of course: one of St Philip's Oratory fathers, Blessed Juvenal Ancina, was made bishop of Saluzzo in Piedmont, much against his will. He set to work to carry out the reforms of Trent, on the model of St Charles, and was poisoned for his pains by a friar who objected to being reformed. Blessed Juvenal lived long enough to forgive his murderer, and by his death achieved the improvement he had been aiming at in his life.

Counsellor of Popes

St Philip did not stop with bishops and cardinals, he became at the end of his life the **Counsellor of Popes**. The last few Popes of the sixteenth century were all in one way or another followers of Philip, and he did not hesitate to advise them as he thought fit. He behaved towards them with remarkable informality, and they did not seem to mind. Clement VIII in particular was very willing for Philip to sit down in his presence and keep his hat on - though he made no secret of the fact that he would like him to exchange it for a red one. Philip all his life long was a lover of freedom and independence of action, cultivating a certain eccentricity, combined with an abstraction of manner, that endeared him to others, perhaps especially because it was an age of formality and etiquette. On occasion, when his followers found him stubborn, they resorted to getting the Pope to give him direct orders, but Philip was equal even to that. When Clement VIII ordered him to stay in bed and not to hear confessions in church, because of his age and ill health, he sent two amazingly cheeky notes, in which he accuses the Pope of neglecting to come and see him, though

Our Lord himself was a frequent visitor. The Pope replied in equally bantering tone that Philip did not deserve a visit because he would not accept the cardinalate so many times offered. Philip was able to use this familiarity with the Pope to good effect at the very end of his life when he persuaded him to accept the good faith of King Henry of Navarre and so permit him to become Henry IV of France, thus putting an end to the wars of religion. Clement VIII needed some persuasion, because the Spanish Ambassador was putting enormous pressure on him to block that outcome, for purely political reasons.

Voice of Prophecy

It is particularly in connection with the Papacy that we hear of St Philip as a **Voice of Prophecy**. Several times he predicted the outcome of papal elections, which were frequent in those days. On other occasions we hear that he could be confident in foretelling the outcome of an illness, though he himself warned against making such predictions. One particularly vivid occasion is recorded, when he was gifted with a sudden insight into what was happening at a distance. During the reign of one of the great reforming Popes, Paul IV, the Jesuits tried to get the Pope to condemn the life and teachings of the Dominican preacher Jerome Savonarola. Saint Philip had been brought up to revere his memory as that of a saint, and joined with the Dominicans in Rome at storming heaven with their prayers. During a night of exposition, St Philip apparently drifted off into a state of abstraction, eventually coming round with a start, to tell them that the cause was won, and the teachings of Savonarola had been approved, as afterwards proved to be the case. It was doubtless because he himself had some experience of the spirit of prophecy that he was quick to detect frauds and self-publicists, who were teeming in Rome at the time. His instinct was always to be suspicious of any claims to supernatural insight, and when asked to examine particular cases could be quite severe. The genuinely holy always thrive under severe examination, and the true prophet is never abashed by honest scepticism; just as St Teresa was confirmed in her vocation by the doubts her advisors raised, so the Venerable Orsula Benincasa meekly tolerated Philip's harsh interrogation to prove the genuineness of her spiritual life. The frauds objected loudly to being found out.

Man of Primitive Times

Part of St Philip's originality lay in his radical sympathy with the early Church, which led to his title of **Man of Primitive Times**. During the sixteenth century a number of fanatics had disturbed the faith of many by introducing strange ideas and practices which they claimed were those of the 'primitive church'. St Philip took the trouble to find out what the early Church was really like, partly by reading the works of the great writers of the past, the Fathers, and partly by his exploration of the relics of early Christianity in the catacombs. Two of his followers, Bozio and Baronio, were to take up this lead and become the greatest exponents of early Christian history and archaeology. The catacombs, long forgotten, were opened up and explored by Bozio, who discovered the paintings, carvings and inscriptions that demonstrated what early Christian worship was like, while Baronio, at St Philip's orders, studied Church History in great depth, eventually producing the thirteen vast volumes of his Annals, to show, year by year, what really happened. St Philip was not a scholar like those two, but he knew well enough the value of the truth about early Christianity. It was, for instance, in the pages of John Cassian that he found the practice of frequent confession and communion, which was such a feature of his teaching.

Winning Saint

It was above all in hearing confessions that St Philip won his title of **winning saint**. He exercised the most remarkable attraction towards people of all ages and classes, but particularly the young. Part of his charm was that he accepted people as they were, sins and all, and was able to lead them gently on to where they should be, rather than beginning by confronting them directly with their wickedness. His follower Saint Francis de Sales used to repeat the proverb that you can catch more flies with a spoonful of honey than with a bucketful of vinegar. The sweetness of Philip's manner meant that sinners felt comfortable approaching him, and the gentle good humour of his advice and counselling enabled them, to their own eternal amazement, to break free from sins in a manner which they never thought possible. Many were brought by friends to hear Philip preach, or to take part in the afternoon exercises called the Oratory, with no intention of doing more than enjoy the music and the experience, once only. But they found they were unable to stop themselves going back again and again, until somehow they found they were making their confession to St Philip, who never seemed at all surprised at what they had to say, and often helped them along by telling them what their difficulties were. This became, indeed, a characteristic of his followers, notably St Francis de Sales, as we have mentioned. Fathers of the Oratory have always encouraged frequent confession, and found that by copying St Philip's gentle approach they have been able to bring many wanderers back to Christian faith and practice. Newman and Faber had extraordinary success in winning over the poor workers of nineteenth-century Birmingham and London, while Blessed Sebastian Valfré of the Turin Oratory was even able to make progress with the princely family of Savoy. Blessed Sebastian was also very effective in helping prisoners of war, and on one occasion received a delegation of Dutch Calvinists to thank him for his generous and humane treatment of protestant prisoners, even though that very gentleness had resulted in many being reconciled to the Catholic Church.

Hidden Hero

St Philip was no publicist: he is called the **Hidden Hero**. One of his mottoes is *amare nesciri*, 'love to be unknown', and like all saints he hated being admired. To this end he cultivated a frivolous manner, verging sometimes on buffoonery, so that the pompous and dignified clergy and nobility of the age might dismiss him and ignore him. When foreign visitors came to admire the saint, he was found reading comic books and laughing aloud. Even during great ceremonies he liked to defuse the occasion by doing something ludicrous like stroking the beards of the Swiss Guards. Some of his fooleries might have the effect of drawing attention to him, but he made sure that it was never an admiring attention. What is more, he expected his followers to imitate him in deflecting admiration. Particularly the more serious, the learned, the well-born, might find that Philip expected them to play leap-frog in the streets, take his revolting little dog Capriccio for a walk, or sing comic songs at polite gatherings. The sober historian Baronio was often the butt of these jokes, and the naturally buoyant Macaluffi got so tired of having to dance before dignified visitors that he was known to hide when he saw anyone important coming. Much of St Philip's success lay in his policy of concealing how serious his intentions really were. He desperately wanted to lead people to a greater love of God and neighbour, and found that an appearance of frivolity could win them over and reform them unawares.

The enemies of the Church never took him seriously enough to realise what a threat he constituted. The same thing has happened since, in different ways: the Oratorians have rather cultivated an appearance of frivolity to deflect attack, and to win people over without them realising it. A cheerful and light-hearted answer does more to win people than serious earnestness. When Saint Luigi Scrosoppi was collecting for his orphanage, he was savagely struck by one angry anti-clerical. The saint's response was to say, 'Well, that was clearly intended for me, but what are you going to give my orphans?'

Sweetest of Fathers

This character of Philip led Newman to call him also the **Sweetest of Fathers**. Sweetness is a difficult characteristic to appreciate: it can so often seem nauseating and sickly. As a rule anyone who sets out to be 'sweet' is bound to appear repulsive. Perhaps St Philip's 'sweetness' meant really that he cared about other people, and wanted them to be happy. Not that he wanted them to like him - he could be quite off-putting when confronted with hero-worship. At times he was brusque, especially when dealing with gushing women, or importunate saints. Yet behind it, those who took the trouble to look found a soul that did actually care. That is why St Charles Borromeo was not put off by the rather harsh letters St Philip sent him, nor by Philip's prevarication and eventual refusal to send any of his men to found an Oratory in Milan. Nor were Talpa and Tarugi, the pioneers of the Naples Oratory, put off by the same hesitation and prevarication the saint displayed towards their plans. They might shout at each other occasionally, as on the famous occasion when Talpa snatched a letter out of St Philip's hands, but underneath they knew always that his affection and his concern was genuine. In his old age he inspired an extraordinary devotion, and young men competed with cardinals to serve him. He was always surrounded by a cloud of listeners, who hardly left him alone for a moment, hanging on his words, joining in his prayers, helping him with his illnesses, even trying to protect him from others who arrived with exactly the same intentions. In a word, people loved him.

Flower of Purity

Not that they were without good reason. Much of his loveableness came from the fact that he was, in Newman's words, a **Flower of Purity**. Real purity, that unfashionable virtue, always has the effect of making people most attractive. The sixteenth century, at least in the early decades, was an age that thought it had grown out of purity, decency, and Christian morality: that was one of the effects of the worst excesses of the 'renaissance', a deliberate revival of paganism that began with poetry and ended in depravity. St Philip stood out against his age, until his age at last caught up with him.

Without being prurient or repressive, he was able to help people confront their difficulties in sexuality, and overcome their obsessions. Many of the young men who came to him had become enslaved by habits they did not believe they could break. St Philip did not rebuke them or discourage them by stark confrontation, but taught them to pray, taught them to love, and showed them how much God loved them. Once he elicited the desire to want to change their lives, the actual change seems to have come very easily. The great Tarugi long resisted him, because he found himself unable to break off a sinful relationship of long standing. St Philip did not hurry him, but after a while brought him to the point that once that relationship had ended naturally (as they always do), Tarugi was perfectly content to spend the rest of his life in chastity, and died a Cardinal. (In this case the relationship actually ended because the lady died, but the point is that Tarugi did not feel the need to go and find another.) Others found that when they came to confession to St Philip, the mere contact with him was enough to liberate them from the entanglements that so perplexed them. Listening to the beating of his heart, they found there a real love, which drove out whatever was sordid or distorted in their lives. As a result many of his young men were able to undertake lives of celibacy in the service of the Church, while others made good Christian marriages and extended St Philip's influence to the next generation.

Martyr of Charity

The secret was that St Philip was also a **Martyr of Charity**. We find in the writings of St Francis de Sales the spiritual and moral teaching that St Philip himself never wrote down, and it is clear from them that the key to chastity is charity. Charity means above all the love of God, which inevitably finds expression in the love of neighbour. The love of God on our part is our natural response to our realisation of the love God has for us. That is the fruit of prayer, both private and liturgical: in prayer we hear God telling us how much he loves us, and filled with the knowledge of that love, we find love to spare for others. That is why the test of whether we love God is applied by examining whether we love other people. When St Philip began the afternoon meetings he called the Oratory, they were designed to fill his young audience with the realisation of the love of God. He then sent them around the city to put that love into action in practical work for the poor and the sick. But despite all these loving intentions, there were many who disapproved of what St Philip was doing, and made their disapproval felt. He lived for many years in the *convito* of San Girolamo, a loosely-organised community of priests, under the direction of a lay confraternity. The confraternity's deputy, a doctor called Vincenzo Teccosi, strongly disapproved of St Philip, and did everything he could to make his life difficult, persuading the church sacristans to be obstructive and unco-operative as only sacristans can. St Philip endured years of this persecution to such effect that Teccosi himself was won over, and ended as one of the saint's devout followers. But there were greater perils to come, after St Philip had become well known as the inspiration of many young followers. The great work of reform in the Church, in its early phases, involved a hard critical look at anything that seemed to threaten Christian unity, and all sorts of groups came under suspicion of being divisive. St Philip was more than once reported to the various commissions around the Pope, and at one time was ordered to put a stop to his public meetings and walks around the city. He meekly obeyed, and was quickly rewarded in each case with a message of confidence from the Pope himself.

Heart of Fire

St Philip is depicted in art, and symbolised in the decoration of Oratory churches everywhere, with the device of a **Heart of Fire**. It was in the heart that the saint particularly felt the heat of God's love, and as we shall see, there were mystical and even physical reasons for this. Others could feel the warmth of Philip's heart, and there were many who claimed that when they were troubled or distressed they only had to lay their head to Philip's heart to find consolation. There is obviously a connection with the devotion to the Sacred Heart of Jesus, which was already familiar in St Philip's time. The heart is conceived as the centre not only of love but of goodwill, good intention: the Heart of Jesus is His human love for us, His intention for our good. When St Margaret Mary Alacoque had those visions that spread devotion to the Sacred Heart into the frigid waste of Jansenist France, she was already prepared for them by the writings of St Francis de Sales, (who founded her order of the Visitation) who in turn learnt warmth from the heart of Philip. St Francis probably never met St Philip in this life, though they are often shown together in paintings, but he was very familiar with the Oratory, knew Blessed Juvenal Ancina intimately, and began to found Oratories in France before he was whisked off to become a bishop. It was a phrase in the writings of St Francis that gave Newman the idea for his motto, 'Heart speaks to Heart'. The heart of St Philip spoke to the Sacred Heart of Jesus, as well as to the hearts of his followers.

Discerner of Spirits

We are told by St Paul that one of the most important gifts of the Holy Spirit is that of being a **Discerner of Spirits**. We have already touched on St Philip's instinctive awareness of truth and righteousness, and of his gift of prophecy which enabled him to discern the difference between genuine and false mysticism. In more ordinary matters, too, he was discerning, particularly on the question of a man's vocation. He was far from being a recruiter for his own institute, but advised his young men on which of the many available religious orders they should join, sending many to the Dominicans and the Capuchins, and some even to the Jesuits. Although the latter were fundamentally different in tone, organisation and mission from the Oratory, St Philip and St Ignatius could understand each other, and St Philip knew that different types of spirituality suit different people. It was Ignatius who compared Philip to a bell, sending many people into the Church but itself remaining outside, though St Philip knew quite clearly that his freedom-loving spirit could never fit into the Jesuit mould. He felt much more at home with the Dominicans at the church of Santa Maria sopra Minerva, and helped in the training of their novices, while bringing his own youths frequently into the Dominican church for the divine office. Following the tradition of Cassian (which survives in the Benedictines, notably in the school of the Blessed Columba Marmion) St Philip was a great believer in leading every person to God in the way that suited them best. He treated each one as an individual, knowing instinctively what sort of mortification would be of the greatest benefit, what sort of prayer would be most fruitful, what sort of practical charitable work would most bring out the love of God and neighbour.

Choicest of Priests

Although greatly appreciative of the value of lay sanctity, St Philip was the **Choicest of Priests**. He came late to the priesthood, not ordained until he was nearly thirty-six, after he had already fulfilled a useful lay vocation. Ordained just in time before the introduction of the seminary, which he would have found stifling, he established himself as a priest in the most independent way possible. From the beginning he saw the priesthood as consisting essentially of three things, prayer, preaching and the celebration of the sacraments. Even in his time there were many who saw it predominantly as a fund-raising and administrative post, and one of the reasons there was opposition to him at first was his insistence on hearing confessions regularly and celebrating Mass daily at a convenient time for the people, thus putting to shame those priests who did neither. Preaching was even frowned upon in some circles, because it could so easily lead to divisions and party rivalries, and St Philip's easy familiar style of speaking seemed hardly reverent in an age used to grand rhetoric, extravagant gestures and dramatic pauses. The exercise of the Oratory was predominantly one of preaching, but it led inevitably to the Confessional, and to the frequent reception of Communion. Without prayer, none of that would have been possible, and throughout his life St Philip spent long periods in prayer, being faithful in celebrating the entire Divine Office, often in company with others.

Mirror of the divine life

It was through prayer that St Philip became the **Mirror of the divine life**. The human soul is designed to be a mirror to reflect the love of God into the world. The various exercises of penance are designed to polish that mirror. St Philip believed strongly in the value, indeed the necessity, of that polishing process, but he did not believe in it being too abrasive. Many in that age took penances to extremes, practising mortifications that seem bizarre. Some, such as 'taking the discipline' (self flagellation) were so wide-spread that they can be considered the sixteenth-century equivalent of jogging, uncomfortable and undignified exercise that is supposed to be good for you, so common as to be quite normal. St Philip did not abolish this practice, but limited it, and considered it of very little use compared with the two really important forms of mortification which he taught. One was the 'mortification of the reasoning process', meaning that they should try to check that pride in their own brightness which was such a snare at that period. Cleverness, science, education, were all good things, but once you began to think they made you important they could be very destructive. That is why St Philip gave Baronio a hard time while he was writing his Annals, affecting to think they were unimportant. Baronio was given no time off to write; he was asked to pay his living expenses with the money set aside for printing; when he presented St Philip with a finished volume the saint tossed it aside and asked Baronio to go and serve Mass. As a result the Venerable Baronio became a very holy man himself. The other means of mortification, which St Philip called the greatest, was life in community. In order to perpetuate the work of the Oratory, St Philip allowed some of his priest followers to form a community, living together without the vows taken by monks or other religious. In that common life they found all the mortifications they needed: again Baronio seems to have born the brunt of it, complaining that it always seemed to be his turn to cook.

Pattern of Humility

As a result of all that polishing, St Philip inevitably became a **Pattern of Humility**. The light he shed on the world was not his own, as he knew very well, but the light of Christ. This meant that even when extraordinary things happened at his hands he had no difficulty in recognising that they were God's work, not his. When someone made a fatuous remark about the great things saints do, St Philip said, 'don't say that, say rather that God does great things through his saints'. He had a catchphrase in his early years, 'when are we going to begin to do good?' but in later life he lamented that he himself had never got round to doing any good at all. He had no confidence at all in himself, but was absolutely confident in the grace of God. That meant that he could be at times imperious and autocratic in his government of the Oratory community, knowing that what he insisted on was not his own prejudice but the will of God. He could also lay his hands on the sick and watch them recover, and do other such things, without imagining that it was in any sense his own power at work. Humility is an indispensable qualification for being a saint, and true humility includes knowing when you are right, and when is the proper occasion to let God work miracles through you.

Example of Simplicity

His humility brought him also to be an **Example of Simplicity**. This was particularly manifest in the style he adopted for preaching, and which he expected his followers to adopt. Instead of dazzling his hearers with science, he spoke very simply about the love of God. At the afternoon Oratory there were commonly four discourses, one on the life of a saint, one on some aspect of Christian virtue (often delivered by a child), one on the history of the Church (this was Baronio's speciality), and one commenting on some passage from Scripture, Cassian or some other book. The commentary originally took the form of an unscripted dialogue between two of the young men, discussing in public what the text might mean. Tarugi was the one who excelled at this technique. All the speakers, even Baronio, were expected to keep their words simple and to the point. They did not speak standing up on a rostrum, in vestments, but wore their ordinary cassocks and sat down with the people. Only when the numbers attending got too large was there a raised platform for the speakers to sit on. Inevitably as the Oratory grew more popular the informality of the first days was lost, but even after St Philip's death the exercises still displayed the simple familiarity which so charmed John Evelyn when he visited Rome in 1644. In his contacts with people St Philip maintained that simple manner which made him equally at home with Popes and beggars, and he took a mischievous delight in shocking the dignified. One of his particular friends was Saint Felix of Cantalice, a very simple Franciscan lay brother who used to wander the streets collecting alms for the friary, and was despised by polite society as a disgrace to the cloth. St Philip and St Felix understood one another very well, and used to enjoy swapping hats, or drinking out of the same bottle like vagrants. St Charles Borromeo found it difficult to hide his displeasure when he discovered that St Philip had consulted St Felix and accepted his advice over the rule which the cultivated aristocrat Charles had written for his own version of an Oratory community.

Light of Holy Joy

Above all else, St Philip is remembered as a **Light of Holy Joy**. Much of his charm derived from the fact that he seemed to be able to radiate joy around him, making it appear really possible to 'serve the Lord in gladness' as the psalm puts it. (*Ps 99:2*) Even in his illnesses, and when he and his work were under attack, he continued to preserve a joyful countenance. It is true that some of his portraits make him look rather severe, but those who knew him well always complained that none of the portraits did him justice, and the artists had distorted their impression by making him look the way they thought a saint ought to

look. His friends said that he always had a twinkle in his
eye which no painter could capture. That joy was especially
noticeable when he said Mass. Although he encouraged the
grand and solemn ceremonial Masses, with music by his
friends Palestrina or Animuccia, because he knew that these
attracted people, his own preference was always to say
Mass simply, without singing, the last Mass of the day. His
delight in receiving and distributing Communion were
much in evidence. Towards the end of his life he usually
said Mass in his own little chapel with only one or two
servers, and allowed his delight in the Lord to prolong his
thanksgiving after Communion to the extent that the servers
used to slip out for an hour or so and leave him to it. On
these occasions he might break out into singing
unexpectedly, chanting a Gloria or an Alleluia. He was also
observed to rise to the tips of his toes from time to time, and
on occasion some were convinced he actually left the floor,
so eager was he to strain upwards to the source of all joy.
He was always encouraging others to share his joy, in the
Mass, in prayer, in music, in explaining the goodness of
God. He was moreover happy to encourage sports and
picnics, which the reformers of the age thought frivolous. A
major difference between St Philip and his hero Savonarola,
is that while both encouraged their followers to bring
musical instruments to their meetings, Savonarola had them
burnt, and Philip had them played. During his spring or
summer walking pilgrimages around the seven great

churches of Rome, he would organise a lavish picnic in some vineyard, to be accompanied by a group of musicians and singers. Even on his winter walks in the city he would startle the more dignified of his followers by suddenly proposing a race, or leaping down flights of steps four at a time. There seems to have been a natural ebullience which escaped him unexpectedly from time to time. There were those who were shocked; there were more who found the joy infectious and joined in.

Image of Childhood

Perhaps the secret was that he remained an **Image of Childhood**. Unlike so many people, St Philip never forgot that he had once been a boy, and retained a sympathy for children of the same age that he had been himself. As a result noisy small boys clustered round him to the extent that his older followers found intolerable. As usual, it was poor Baronio who had most to complain about, finding his studies interrupted by the racket they were making. St Philip's reply is famous: 'as long as they don't sin, they can chop wood on my back for all I care.' However to give Baronio a break he usually took them outside whenever possible, letting them get on with some game while he prayed, or taught some of them to pray. He and his followers never took to providing formal education, perhaps because the regimentation necessary in a school was alien to St Philip's independent spirit, but in later ages Oratories have been associated with schooling to a large extent. The Oratory in France, in particular, which took a rather different form from elsewhere, became famous for running schools, producing philosophers of the calibre of Malebranche, and alumni with the flair of Robespierre. Newman and Faber both started schools in the English Oratories, and although the complexities of modern education means that schools need to be run by professionals, there is still a Philippine presence in the remaining Oratory schools.

Picture of Old Age

The very old and the very young are often able to understand each other better than those in the middle, so we are not surprised to find that St Philip was also the **Picture of Old Age**. Partly, of course, this is because we know more about him in old age than at any other time of his life. Almost as soon as he died the process of Canonisation was set in motion, which involved taking depositions from anyone who cared to testify to his life and character. The surviving evidence includes innumerable anecdotes told by those alive at his death, very largely about things that had happened only a year or so before. Again, it was only in old age that he became sufficiently famous for people to want his portrait painted. Not that St Philip approved of that - portraits had to be done surreptitiously, worked up from sketches done when the artists thought he wasn't looking. (This shyness of being painted extended to some of his followers: Saint Luigi Scrosoppi, despite living into the age of photography, managed to escape ever being snapped. Newman, in contrast, absolutely loved having his photograph taken, and sitting for portraits.) Actually St Philip was not all that old when he died, not quite eighty, but he was in poor health, and had given the impression for years of being at his last gasp. What was noticeable was that he remained in good humour, and was pleasant to visit, without the distasteful crotchetiness so common among the infirm and elderly. The phrase 'what a beautiful old man!' is recorded on the lips of one who saw him for the first time.

Director of Souls

The art of all arts, as St Gregory said, is to be a **Director of Souls**. There is no work more important, and no work more dangerous in unskilled hands. St Ignatius attempted to provide a universal pattern for guiding the spiritual life, though he insisted that a skilled and wise director was also necessary. St Philip, without having a pre-arranged pattern to follow, did at least have the wisdom and skill necessary. This is an aspect of that discernment of spirits we have noticed already. The truth is that, as Our Lord warned us very clearly, the way to salvation is narrow and hedged about with difficulties. A false step can be disastrous, and the wrong spiritual advice catastrophic. St John of the Cross, when he attempted to complete his great series of books by describing the perfection of contemplation, in the *Living Flame of Love*, found he had to spend most of the book warning about the perils on the way, of which the greatest, he tells us, is the spiritual director. That St Philip was able to lead so many people on the way of salvation shows that he was a better director than most. There were failures of course - even Our Lord did not succeed with all his listeners - but there were also rather a lot of successes. That the late sixteenth century was an age of saints is largely due to St Philip, and we have already mentioned some of his Venerable, Blessed and Saintly companions and followers.

Gentle Guide of Youth

For many it began when they first met St Philip as the **Gentle Guide of Youth**. Although men and women of all ages and ranks flocked around him, his first and most characteristic work was with young men, beginning in his own youth as one of them. In his early twenties he made a point of seeking out men of his own age, from his own country, employed in the busy commercial quarter of the Banchi, and with time on their hands after work finished at about one or two in the afternoon. (It is not clear why it is always considered an example of papal corruption that the Roman people, of all classes, were able to get through their working day in the morning and not need to work at all after dinner. A few years before, St Thomas More had pointed out, in *Utopia*, that if everyone did a fair share of the work, no one would ever need to do more than a few hours a day.) The time could be used for mischief; St Philip encouraged them to use it for growing in the love of God and neighbour. He began, in other words, on the principle of being an apostle to his equals, but he never neglected that vulnerable but important age group. Bad habits acquired in youth, he pointed out, are difficult to shake off, whereas good ones can grow and form a lifelong character. Hence the development of those afternoon and evening Oratory exercises, to provide a pleasant and instructive way of filling the long hours of freedom. That is why, also, the exact form of St Philip's Oratory could not be duplicated in other lands, where working conditions were harsher, and the time available more restricted. Nevertheless when Newman and Faber began in the industrial cities of England they successfully gathered huge crowds for Oratory exercises after the factory whistle blew in the evening. The continued growth of the Oratory idea stems from this practice of beginning with young people. Obviously as they get older, become established at work and in marriage, there is less leisure for spiritual exercises, but if the foundation is well laid, the habits of prayer and charity inculcated in bachelor days could enleaven the whole family. And out of the many who followed St Philip in youth, a reasonable proportion went on to dedicate their lives to the service of God and man, in religious life, the secular priesthood, or even among the Fathers of the Oratory. St Philip's first priests were three of his young men, Bordini, Baronio, and Alessandro Fedeli, who went to begin the simple community life together at San Giovanni. Many others were to follow, though as ever there was a constant complaint that there were not enough, and the Popes did not help when they kept taking the best ones away to make them bishops. A few years after St Philip's death, two of those he had begun to train as young men were made cardinals, Tarugi and Baronio, and the latter was actually elected Pope in 1605, though he got away with refusing to accept office.

Patron of thine Own

From the earliest days when St Philip first began to encourage his fellow youths in Rome until today, he is invoked as the **Patron of thine Own**. All members of religious institutes have a feeling that their founders belong to the family in a special way, but perhaps St Philip more than most is remembered as the father of every Oratorian community. The Oratory, meaning the afternoon exercises of prayer and instruction for lay people, particularly the young, was very much his own invention, often imitated, never emulated. Crowds of men, and women as well, over the last four centuries have been formed or helped by attending these meetings, which take different forms in different places at different ages. Sometimes there is a formal membership with enrolled 'Brothers of the Secular

Oratory', or some such title, at other times there is a simpler feeling of belonging. In whatever form the Oratory ('Secular' or 'Little' Oratory) takes, there is always a feeling that we are trying to do for our time and place what St Philip did for the Rome of the sixteenth century. The communities of priests who exist to guide and direct these Oratory exercises, the 'Congregations' of the Oratory, are very much modelled on the one St Philip set up at Santa Maria in Vallicella, again with local and period variations. Because there is the minimum of institutional structure, each house in some way feels directly dependent on St Philip, and he is spoken of in a familiar way as the guiding spirit behind whatever the Fathers are trying to do. Newman is often considered a second founder, or the one who rescued the Oratory institute from the chaos of the nineteenth century, but he is not the patron in anything like the same way. It is not for love of Newman that men join the Oratory, or if they do they do not persevere: it is for love of St Philip. Newman and Faber, the venerable, beatified and canonised members of the Institute, all have their place in the affection of members, but none come close to the position of St Philip.

Hospes Anglorum

There is one more title which Newman gives our saint, only in the Latin version of the litany: he is **Hospes Anglorum**. Most translations assume there is a misprint here, and translate it as 'guest of the angels', but

Newman knew what he was doing, and the phrase actually means 'host of the English'. St Philip lived for thirty years at the *convito* of San Girolamo, directly opposite the then gate of the English College in Rome. The tradition to which Newman refers is that he knew the English students well, and used to greet them with the opening line of the hymn for the Holy Innocents, *Salvete flores martyrum*, 'Hail, flowers of martyrs'. For this was the age when the newly-ordained priests returned to face persecution and the ever-present threat or promise of martyrdom. It is reported that before leaving the College each would make his way to San Girolamo to ask a blessing from the Apostle of Rome, all except one who disdained to go and afterwards fell away from the faith. Certainly it was impossible for the students to live in that corner of Rome without being aware of what St Philip was doing, impossible for St Philip not to take an interest in these young heroes. But frustratingly there is little contemporary evidence of contact between them. The English College was run by Jesuits, who did not encourage the students to go out and mix with the Romans, and it is unlikely they would have been permitted to attend the Oratory exercises, which were, after all, primarily intended for layfolk. But even if St Philip could not welcome them into his home, we can be sure that he welcomed them into his heart, and that he took an interest in England, at that time so oppressed and

so unhappy. One of Newman's hymns to St Philip
invokes him as leaving Rome after his death and
travelling across Europe, in the person of his Institute:

> He travelled, and he travelled on,
> He crossed the swelling sea,
> He sought our island's very heart,
> And here at length is he!

Philip Neri celebrating Mass.

THE LIFE OF SAINT PHILIP

We have seen what sort of a person St Philip was, and what influence he had on those around him; now it is time to look at the course of his life. Newman continues his litany with a series of biographical intercessions, which we may continue to use as a framework.

Who didst observe chastity in thy youth

It was remarkable in those days for a young person even to want to be chaste, let alone to achieve it. Our hero spent his childhood and adolescence in Florence, during the last flowering of the Renaissance, that glamorous but fundamentally flawed attempt to revive ancient paganism in behaviour as well as art and literature. Born on 21 July 1515, he was educated in the Dominican school at San Marco, still visited for the glorious frescoes of Fra Angelico, and the compelling memory of Savonarola. In old age St Philip used to say to his Dominican friends, 'all the good in me comes from the Fathers of San Marco'. They certainly inspired him with a profound love of prayer, and an uncompromising determination to put God before the values of this world. It was less than a generation since the death of Savonarola, and the controversies of his time were very much alive. In the bewildering political changes of those years, St Philip and the Dominicans were obviously on the side of the republicans against the tyranny of the Medici family. All his life Philip preserved a longing for freedom, and independence of thought and action, which he found, as all saints do, to lie in conformity with the love of God, rather than being swept away by the mood of the hour, the fashion of the moment, the political climate, or the pressure of his contemporaries. In other words, in opting for chastity, he was making a radical choice to be different from others of his age.

We need not assume that this independent stance came easily. It took courage and determination, and we can deduce from his advice to others how he himself had grown. Stories told about him as a young man in Rome illustrate this. There were two principal means of remaining free: prayer, and avoiding the occasion of sin. Once when some contemporaries had trapped Philip in the company of two or three dubious ladies, he simply fell to prayer, and eventually embarrassed the poor creatures to the extent that they unlocked the door themselves and let him go. Another time, a famous courtesan lured him to her den by pretending to be ill and desirous of repentance, but when he saw through her ruse he simply got up and left, leaving her to vent her rage by throwing furniture at him. Until late in life he was careful never to be alone with a woman, and always insisted that his priests should hear the confessions of women and children in church, and through a grille. Simply keeping away from risky circumstances, and becoming so accustomed to prayer that it was second nature to pray in times of temptation, seemed to be the answer. That, and charity, which as we have seen, is the key to all virtues. St Philip never considered himself superior to those who had fallen into sin of any kind, and warned his followers that anyone who lacked sympathy and understanding for sinners was bound to fall himself in the same way. St Philip helped many young men to achieve freedom from sin because he never trusted himself.

Who didst seek Rome by divine guidance

Although he always remained a Florentine at heart, St Philip left his native city as a teenager, never to return. Possibly as a result of a decline in family fortunes after the return of the Medici in 1531, or possibly because he could not endure to live under a tyranny, he said goodbye to his father Francesco Neri, his stepmother Lucrezia, and his sisters Caterina and Lisabetta, and set off to seek his fortune. He first made for his uncle Romolo, a merchant at San Germano near Monte Cassino, but he very quickly found that a business career did not suit him, and stayed with the firm only a very short time. There is a strong tradition that at this phase of his life he prayed at the chapel of the Crucifix lodged in a crack in the cliffs near Gaeta. The place is too far from San Germano for regular visits, and may have been a stage on his journey to Rome. It is certainly a dramatic place of prayer, a place where an

impressionable teenager could find himself close to God,
and ponder on his choices in life. On the rocky walls of the
chasm are circles enclosing the letters **yhs**, in the form
used by St Bernadine when he preached the Name of
Jesus; they say St Bernadine carved them himself. St Philip
too was to be afire with the love of Our Lord, and with the
desire to make him known. And so he came to Rome.

Who didst hide so long in the Catacombs

He hit Rome, unknown and unemployed, at the age of
eighteen or nineteen. His Florentine nationality was enough
to find him a job as tutor to the two sons of a Florentine
merchant, who gave him a room and an allowance. He spent
his ample spare time partly in attending lectures in theology
and philosophy, and partly in beginning those famous walks
around Rome, meeting his contemporaries and asking them
when they were going to begin to do good. After a few
years' study he sold his books and became a sort of urban
hermit. He lived extremely simply, but was able to be on
good terms with the people around him, young professionals
working in the banks, as well as the poor and destitute of
Rome. A hermit is to a certain extent classless. He attended
Mass and the Office in different churches, but naturally felt
at home with the Dominicans at the Minerva church, where
Fra Angelico is buried. And at night he began to explore the
relics of ancient Christianity, particularly at the catacomb of
San Sebastiano outside Rome. Newman exaggerates when

he says Philip 'hid' in the catacombs: he was constantly seen around the streets of Rome, but he does appear to have spent the night sometimes in prayer underground. The catacombs were surprisingly little known at this period, simply called the 'grottoes', and not considered a place of pilgrimage. It was only later, after the researches of St Philip's followers the Bozii brothers, that they were explored. The young saint probably did not go very far in, he was there to pray in union with the first Christians, the martyrs of Rome, not to archaeologise. He retained his love for the catacombs and other early Christian sites of Rome all his life, and for years led great crowds on the day-long walk between the seven great pilgrimage churches.

Who didst receive the Holy Ghost into thy heart

It was in the catacomb of San Sebastiano that he had this extraordinary experience. At Pentecost in 1544, while deep in prayer, he became aware of the action of the Holy Spirit, in the fire of his love, which he could feel localised in his heart. Only at the end of his life did he tell anyone about this, and his confidant Pietro Consolini waited until 1643 before telling anyone else. Yet the experience was not without precedent: the prophet Jeremiah cries out that 'I feel a fire burning within me, imprisoned in my heart'. (*Jer 20:9*) Several spiritual writers have described this experience of feeling fire in the heart, the *incendium amoris*, notably the fourteenth-century English mystic Richard Rolle. What St

Philip told Consolini is that it was as if a ball of fire entered his mouth and lodged in his heart. St Teresa described the same experience as like being pierced with a burning arrow, and the scar was reported to be visible on her heart after her death. Blessed Antonio Grassi, a priest of the Oratory at Fermo, felt it as being struck by lightning, and bore a visible scar under his left eye for the rest of his life. In St Philip's case too there was a visible physical trace, in that his heart was actually enlarged to the extent that the ribs were forced outward, and it palpitated violently on occasion. Pope Benedict XIV describes the condition as an 'aneurism' which gives it a name but explains nothing. The reality seems to be that an intense spiritual awareness of the love of God, a deep experience of what it means to be loved by God, can have a lasting physical effect on the body. The palpitation was certainly very noticeable during St Philip's lifetime, and many witnesses speak about it. He himself had no hesitation in attributing it to the Holy Spirit, and would press people to his heart when they were disturbed or distressed. In feeling that extraordinary palpitation, they never failed to find comfort. The feeling of warmth remained with St Philip too, and he could not bear overheated rooms, walking lightly clad even in the coldest weather (and Rome can be really cold at times). Much of St Philip's dynamism and eagerness to proclaim the love of God to all he met stems from this intense awareness of love which he carried about with him at all times.

Who didst experience such wonderful exstacies

From his catacomb period onward it was not uncommon for St Philip to go off into an abstraction, and pass some time apparently unaware of what was going on around him. At times this prevented him from speaking, and towards the end of his life he found public speaking difficult, since he was ever liable to drop into one of these abstractions. But he himself considered them of no significance whatever, except as a useful humiliation, a 'foolery' as he would call it. Indeed it is a commonplace among spiritual writers to make nothing of the odd phenomena which so excite the onlookers. In speaking about others who were gaining a reputation for exstatic mysticism, St Philip was scathing about their 'exstacies' and considered that they were infinitely better off without them. St Teresa took exactly the same attitude, and famously remarked about one exstatic nun, 'make her eat meat, and don't let her pray too much'. (*Letters, 127*) Real saints always have a robust common-sense attitude towards anything that smacks of the extraordinary: they warn us constantly that it is perilous to make anything of the physical phenomena of mysticism, either in oneself or in others. It seems that they are no more than the natural result of a vivid imagination. A morbid or diseased imagination can produce exactly the same phenomena as one that is genuinely holy and in tune with the Holy Spirit. We should not look, therefore, at the phenomena, but at the life and teachings of the person concerned. Humility about oneself, and charity to others remain the only reliable tests of whether someone is really in love with God or not. St Philip passes both tests. His humility has already been mentioned, and is specifically in evidence in his dislike that any one should know about or talk about the 'exstacies', or any other such things. His charity was shown in action from the beginning of his time in Rome.

Who didst so lovingly serve the little ones

Charity towards the 'little ones' of God was his practice, and one he enforced on all who wanted to follow him. This does not only mean children, but the poor and neglected as well, not to mention those who might be great in this world but were very little indeed in the eyes of God. His work as a tutor to the two boys gave him a bare subsistence, but he did the work well, and they grew up to be a credit to him. No doubt he instructed them in reading, writing and arithmetic as he was expected to do, but his real interest was in teaching them to be good Christians. This surely is why he never got involved in regular schooling, in having to organise a secular curriculum to satisfy the demands of parents hoping to send their children into a successful commercial career. St Philip's Oratories have never, in fact, made much of a success at running ordinary schools, and it is usually considered outside the scope of Oratorian fathers. They are more at home, as St Philip was himself, in taking the children out of school for devotions and religious instruction in a form that was more attractive than the chalk of the classroom.

In looking after the poor there was plenty of scope in sixteenth-century Rome, as at all times and all places. Even after relief for the poor and sick was well organised, there were always needs, since the better the facilities there are for the poor, the more new ones arrive in the city to take advantage of them. And in St Philip's early days in Rome there were real problems following the sack of the city only a few years before. In particular the public hospitals had lost their resources to the extent that they were unable to provide more than shelter and basic medical attention; all nursing, washing and feeding had to be done by relations or volunteers. That is why St Philip made such a point of sending his young men to work in the hospitals, setting the fastidious youths to changing sheets and emptying slops. Towards the end of his life conditions had improved, not least because of the work of his disciple St Camillus, and hospital visiting became more a matter of providing human and spiritual comfort, but events like the epidemic of 1591 which killed St Aloysius brought new emergencies. St Philip could also spare attention for the ever-unpopular gypsies of Rome. During an invasion scare the government had the idea of conscripting the male gypsies for the navy, leaving the women and children to fend for themselves. St Philip made a point of intervening, pointing out the injustice of this, and

...se. He incidentally won the war as well, when the ..., dispelled by the victory at Lepanto, attributed even ...enerals to the prayers of St Philip, as well as his friend ~~ot~~ of Pius V. A returning general presented the saint with an odd little souvenir of the battle, an English fifteenth-century alabaster plaque of St John the Baptist, which he had found on a Turkish galleon being worshipped by its very un-Islamic captain: it can still be seen in St Philip's rooms.

Who didst wash the feet of pilgrims

The first organised work of our saint was the Confraternity of the Holy Trinity which he founded for the 1550 Holy Year. As always, huge crowds of pilgrims were expected to come to Rome for the Jubilee, and as always, Rome was unprepared to accommodate them. Many would come on foot, bringing little with them, and would be quite unable to fend for themselves in the busy city. Philip gathered a group of his young friends and formed a fraternity to assist poor pilgrims. In this they were advised by one of the priests living at San Girolamo, Persiano Rosa, who helped them gain official recognition as a Confraternity, and found them a base for their operations. By the beginning of the Jubilee Year they were ready to receive the influx of pilgrims, pious, no doubt, but demanding. The basic needs were shelter, food and hygiene, and after the long walk to Rome the washing of feet was no empty ceremonial as it is today, but a practical work of kindness. Above all else, however, they considered their duty was to pray with the pilgrims, and help them to prepare for their Jubilee confession. According to later reports, they were able to cope with five hundred pilgrims a day, which must have meant that the small group of youths were assisted by a large number of additional volunteers. The confraternity continued after the end of the Holy Year, finding another useful sphere of occupation in helping convalescents, fit enough to escape from the dreadful public hospitals, but not quite fit enough to look after themselves. The Confraternity continued long after St Philip's time, gaining permanent premises, and welcoming an ever increasing number of pilgrims. Each Holy Year many Romans, Popes and Cardinals included, took their turns assisting the work, disguised in those tall hoods which now appear so sinister but were then a handy way of avoiding publicity. A pilgrim never knew whether his feet were being washed by a noble or a nobody, a pauper or the Pope. Although Philip ceased to be directly involved in organising the work, he still turned up to help, and there exists a painting showing him in an apron ladling out soup, looking rather annoyed at the intrusive artist.

Who didst ardently thirst after martyrdom

St Philip moved on. At Persiano Rosa's insistence he was ordained priest, in the summer of 1551, and came to live at San Girolamo, where he came under the influence of that engaging retired bandit Buonsignore Cacciaguerra. The latter was a great promoter of the frequent use of the sacraments, encouraging people to come to confession and Communion several times a week. Saint Philip enthusiastically took up this cause, as well as that of encouraging the worship of the Blessed Sacrament in the Forty Hours Devotion. This as we have seen brought him his first experience of persecution. But he was still in doubt about his own future. This was the age when expanding trade routes brought more of the world into the consciousness of Europe, and the newly-encountered people proved to be eager to hear about the Christian faith. Franciscan and Jesuit missionaries were doing great things in America, Africa and the further reaches of Asia, and their letters home were full of encouraging reports. They also regularly appealed for more volunteers. St Philip and his companions were struck by the idea of following St Francis Xavier to the East Indies, but in their uncertainty went to consult the wisest monks they knew, the Trappists at Tre Fontane. After a pause the message came back, 'Rome is to be your Indies', and St Philip's vocation was settled: he and his followers were to evangelise their own homeland, leaving the more glamourous foreign missions to others. Thus he became the Apostle of Rome, hardly ever leaving the city again. On the whole, Oratorians have followed his example, concentrating on building up the faith in the cities where their houses are founded, though often inspiring their young disciples to take up the more adventurous path. The greatest exception was the important Oratory in Goa, under the leadership of Blessed Joseph Vaz, who undertook the difficult mission in Ceylon (Sri Lanka). The native Catholics there were being brutally persecuted by the Dutch, who blocked access to European missionaries. Indians like Blessed Joseph could pass unobserved, and successfully kept the faith alive, winning the confidence of the local people and their ruler. Tragically, after British influence put a stop to the Dutch repression, the Goa Oratory was suppressed by the Portuguese authorities in one of their bouts of anti-Catholicism, and much of the evidence for this dramatic work was lost. However neither Blessed Joseph nor any of his followers were captured and martyred: for actual Oratorian martyrs we have to look to Mexico in the 1920s, Spain in the 1930s, and Poland in the 1940s. Many were slaughtered out of hatred for the faith, of whom the best known is Mgr Salvio Huix-Miralpeix, bishop of Lleida. He, together with two Polish Oratorians, Fr. Ferdynand Machay of the Tarnów Oratory, and Fr. Jan Mikalkowski of Studzianna, are expected to be beatified in the near future.

Who didst distribute the Daily Word of God

Meanwhile St Philip was discovering his own unprecedented field of work. Continuing his familiar conversations with the youth of Rome, he began by inviting them to meet in his room, and when numbers got too great, in a gantry over an aisle of the church. This upper room became known as the 'Oratory', a place for praying in. The meetings were therefore called the 'exercises in the Oratory', and the name stuck. St Philip had no intention of founding an institute, still less an order, but simply of sharing the Word of God with those who cared to listen. When in 1564 the Florentine community asked St Philip to take charge of their national church, S. Giovanni, he sent a few of his followers as priests to serve it, but with the expectation that they would return to S. Girolamo for the Oratory. The rules he gave them were simple guidelines for community life, no more. It became more complex when the Florentines built a special hall to hold the Oratory exercises, and the whole operation - except St Philip himself and his cat - was transferred there in 1574. This proved unsatisfactory, because the Florentines wanted too much control, and enemies were spreading malicious rumours, so only a year later St Philip got the Pope, Gregory XIII, to grant them the ruinous little church of Santa Maria in Vallicella, where they could run their own affairs, and where over the years they built the great New Church, and the adjacent house, Oratory and library. Still the purpose of the establishment remained the same: to expound the Word of God every day in a form adapted to the hearers. Increasing numbers meant increasing complexity, and in old age St Philip was to sigh for those early gatherings, but so many came to listen, and to act on what they had heard, that the work won the admiration even of those who had most distrusted it at first.

Who didst turn so many hearts to God

That, ultimately, is the most extraordinary thing about St Philip, his ability to win people over, not for himself, but for God. In the process, of course, they came to appreciate him as well, which caused him great embarrassment, but the lasting effect was to bring people back to God. This was a more difficult task than it might seem, considering that the entire population of Rome were supposed to be believers, the vast majority Catholics, and a small but significant minority Jewish. No one admitted to being an atheist, agnostic or free-thinker - but many behaved as if they were. It is vastly more difficult to convert a loose-living nominal Catholic than a conscientious scientific atheist of enquiring mind. St Philip was able to win the confidence of the decadent gilded youth, the vagabond drunkard, the corrupt official, the scoffing libertine. There are innumerable stories of how he met people who were quite determined not to be affected by him, but came only to laugh. Some were even prepared to go through the rigmarole of confession without any intention of either admitting what was really wrong with them, still less of doing anything about it. St Philip could be very direct with them, and tell them bluntly that their confession had been a pack of lies, but what they *should* have mentioned was this, and this. And before they knew what was happening they found themselves making an honest confession and actually wanting to repent. Then there were some who had seriously wandered away from the truth, caught up in the fantastic theories and superstitions of the age. Extraordinary efforts were made to bring them to their senses, but to no avail, until Philip was sent for. In the case of one particularly obstinate fanatic, Giacomo Paleologo, St Philip simply spoke to him about the love of God, and won his repentance at once. Having done that, St Philip then persuaded the Pope to advance Paleologo enough money to meet his immediate needs. With regard to the Jews, St Philip was characteristically generous and understanding, though like all his contemporaries he lived in the hope of bringing them as well to the Catholic faith. His usual approach was to invite them to pray to the God of Abraham, Isaac and Jacob to guide them to the truth. Of those that did become Catholics, several were members of the Oratory community and testified at his cause to the sensitive way he approached them. The canonisation documents are full of stories of how Philip won souls for God, told by the people concerned.

Who didst converse so sweetly with Mary

Like all saints, St Philip was familiar with those who had gone before him in God's service, particularly with Our Lady. He seems to have kept up a sort of running conversation with her, partly by repeating his own special version of the Rosary, the endless repetition of the short prayer, 'Virgin Mary, Mother of God, pray to Jesus for me; O Virgin, O Mother!' She is associated with some of the remarkable stories about him. Cesare Baronio testified that when he was severely ill and thought to be dying, he had a dream in which he saw Philip standing before God and begging for Baronio's life, 'grant me Cesare, I need him!' And then Philip turned to the Virgin Mary and simply asked her to arrange it. Baronio woke to find himself cured. St Philip himself was once cured of a threatening illness when he saw Our Lady enter his room. Gallonio was there and tells the story in great detail, how the dying man suddenly sat up and began to talk to Our Lady, appeared to embrace her, and was then terribly embarrassed when he found that those in the room could see nothing, and hid his head under the bedclothes. The saint was less shy on the occasion when he had a vision that Our Lady alone was supporting a dangerous portion of the old church of the Vallicella as it was being demolished to make way for the new. He sent the clerk of works to investigate at once, who reported that the structure was indeed dangerous, and who was thus able to rescue the ancient image of Our Lady which is now above the high altar of the new church.

Who didst raise the dead

There were innumerable stories of miracles associated with St Philip, both before and after his death, indeed the older lives of the Saint are more about miracles than anything else. Philip himself, as we have seen, discounted them, and when asked would say angrily, 'I know nothing about working miracles'. He knew perfectly well that it is only God who works miracles, through people who may or may not be saints: the Gospels warn us clearly enough that there will be many who can claim to have worked miracles in the name of Christ, but do not know him. (*Matt 7:22*) That is why it is only miracles worked after death that can be accepted as evidence for sanctity. Yet there were plenty of them: people cured immediately on contact with the saint's body, or with his possessions. As in the case of the story about Baronio, a dream can be accepted as evidence of the intercession of a saint, when there is indisputable evidence for an inexplicable cure. The recent remarkable cure of a young man dying of Aids in Zambia is associated with his extraordinary devotion to the new Oratorian Saint, Luigi Scrosoppi, who did appear in a dream immediately before the cure. But the particular story to which Newman refers is one of the most curious, yet best documented, of all. Paolo Massimo, a boy belonging to a family who were particularly friendly with St Philip, died at the age of fourteen, surrounded by friends and family, and after receiving the sacraments from the parish priest, Don Camillo. St Philip arrived half an hour too late. Distressed at missing the boy's death, he prayed, sprinkled holy water, and laid his hands on the boy's head. Paolo opened his eyes, asked for a bottle, conversed with St Philip for a quarter of an hour, and peacefully died again. The Massimo family, several of whom gave sworn testimony about the exact course of events at the canonisation process, still continue to celebrate this apparently pointless miracle, a proof, perhaps, of St Philip's human affection for the whole family and his desire to comfort the parents, rather than being of any benefit to the boy. St Philip's own death came not long after. His health started failing after about 1590, and there were many scares, but the end did not come until 26 May 1595, when he died surrounded by his friends and disciples. Antonio Gallonio who tended him in his last illness wrote a detailed account of the events of that last night. He was buried in his own New Church, and immediately acclaimed by the Roman people as a saint, though the canonisation process dragged on for twenty-seven years. His shrine in the far left corner of the Vallicella church was decorated at the expense of one Nero de' Neri, who claimed to be a relation of his: it remains a much-loved place of pilgrimage today.

Who didst set up thy houses in all lands

The spread of the Oratory, and the foundation of new communities based on St Philip's ideas, was something he himself neither expected nor wanted. As far as he was concerned, the exercises of the Oratory were the response to the needs of Rome in his own time. The community of priests was needed to make sure that the exercises were done adequately: he himself had not thought of joining the community even, but expected to continue to live independently at San Girolamo. It took a Papal command for him to move in and become Provost at the Vallicella.

But his followers had other ideas. Talpa and Tarugi in particular had grand ideas about the Oratory being the leaven that would bring about the reform successively of the Curia, the City, and the World. They insisted on going off to make a new foundation in Naples, on rather more monastic lines. There were endless arguments and discussions with Philip about whether this was a good idea or not. In the event the Naples community was made totally independent of Rome, and the principle was established that each Oratory is a free and self-governing community, owing nothing but the inspiration to the original house in Rome. At the same time groups of priests at San Severino, Bologna and Palermo, asked St Philip's permission to imitate his style, and sent members to live in Rome and study how things were done there, before setting up on their own. St Philip seemed happier with this approach. It was not until 1612 that the Constitutions were finalised, and the pattern set for the next three hundred years: each Congregation of the Oratory, consisting of priests, lay brothers and novices, was to be free and independent, following the common constitutions with particular statutes of its own. Its principal work was always to be the sanctification of the laity, adapting the Oratory Exercises to local conditions. Each house was answerable only to the Holy See, but local bishops had a sort of protective oversight. The idea spread very rapidly, particularly in the various countries of the Italian peninsula, and by the end of the eighteenth century there were some hundred and seventy Oratories, including several in Latin America, as well as the Goa and Ceylon houses we have mentioned. By the end of the nineteenth century there were few survivors, as tyrannical anti-Christian governments in country after country stole the buildings and dispersed the communities. After Garibaldi and his imperialist friends had subjected all the nations of Italy to Piedmontese anti-clericalism, the Oratory was all but wiped out in its homelands. The twentieth-century revival owes as much to Newman and Faber as to Rome. The two Oxford converts visited Rome and Naples respectively, and after some initial experimentation set up their houses in Birmingham and London in 1848-9, preserving what was best of the two oldest Oratories at the very moment when they first came under attack. Revivals and new arrivals spread under their influence. The initial impetus in North America and in Germany came about as a conscious imitation of the English Oratories; and new life came into the Italian, Spanish and Polish houses as conditions became more normal. The Oratory in Mexico actually flourished after the savage persecution in the 1920s, and most of the other Latin American communities increased. At the same time the centralisation of Church organisation which reached its climax in the second Vatican Council and the 1983 Code of Canon Law meant that the old independence came under threat, and an international structure had to be set up to coordinate the Oratories of the world. Nevertheless the Fathers still do not take religious vows, and remain secular priests, owning their own property, and bound together only by the 'bond of charity' as St Philip insisted should always be the case, and each house remains free and self-governing. This has proved a blessing during the years of Communist pressure, when the lack of a central organisation made it difficult for the regime to attack the Oratory as a body, and it has also been the salvation of the Oratorian ideal during the decades of confusion in the Church, since those houses that lost the Oratorian spirit and disintegrated were unable to infect the others.

By 1965 there were fifty three Congregations of the Oratory, in twelve countries; by 2000 there were seventy four in seventeen countries, with a large number of would-be Oratories in process of formation. One of the most spectacular recent foundations is Oudtshoorn in Cape Province (1998), with a particular ministry to the Afrikaans-speaking coloured population. New houses continue to be founded either like Naples, by sending existing fathers to colonise a new city (such as Oxford, 1993), or like San Severino by local priests adopting the Oratory style and taking only advice from an existing house (like Nancy, 1998, or Philadelphia, 2000). It does not appear that St Philip has yet concluded his operations.

FURTHER READING

The earliest record of St Philip's life comes from his contemporaries: a close friend and helper, Antonio Gallonio, published a short life in 1600 (printed in the *Acta Sanctorum* for 26 May), and the evidence given for the Canonisation process was collected and published in four volumes (*Studi e Testi,* vols 191, 196, 205 & 224, Vatican, 1957-63). Unfortunately none of these have been translated into English. Of the many modern lives, the most detailed is *St Philip Neri and the Roman Society of his Times,* by Louis Ponnelle and Louis Bordet, translated by Ralph Kerr of the London Oratory (London 1937); and the most recent *St Philip Neri, the Fire of Joy* by Paul Türks of the Aachen Oratory, translated by Daniel Utrecht of the Toronto Oratory (Edinburgh and New York, 1995). To understand the Oratory, see Raleigh Addington, *The Idea of the Oratory,* London, 1965, and Paschal Murray (ed.), *Newman the Oratorian,* Leominster, 1980. The most recent work on the Oratorian life is that by P. Edoardo Cerrato of the Biella Oratory, *S. Filippo Neri, la sua opera e la sua eredità...,* 2002.

CTS
MEMBERSHIP
◉

We hope you have enjoyed reading this booklet. If you would like to read more of our booklets or find out more about CTS - why not do one of the following?

1. Join our Readers CLUB.
We will send you a copy of every new booklet we publish, - through the post to your address. You'll get 20% off the price too.

2. Support our work and Mission.
Become a CTS Member. Every penny you give will help spread the faith throughout the world. What's more, you'll be entitled to special offers exclusive to CTS Members.

3. Ask for our Information Pack.
Become part of the CTS Parish Network by selling CTS publications in your own parish.

Call us now on 020 7640 0042 or return this form to us at CTS, 40-46 Harleyford Road, London SE11 5AY
Fax: 020 7640 0046 email: info@cts-online.org.uk

❏ I would like to join the *CTS Readers Club*

❏ Please send me details of how to join CTS as a *Member*

❏ Please send me a *CTS Information Pack*

Name:...

Address:..

....

Post Code:...

Phone:..

email address:...

Registered charity no. 218951.
Registered in England as a company limited by guarantee no.57374.